Science Champs

Materials

WRITTEN BY
MANISHA NAYAK

ILLUSTRATED BY
ELIZ ONG

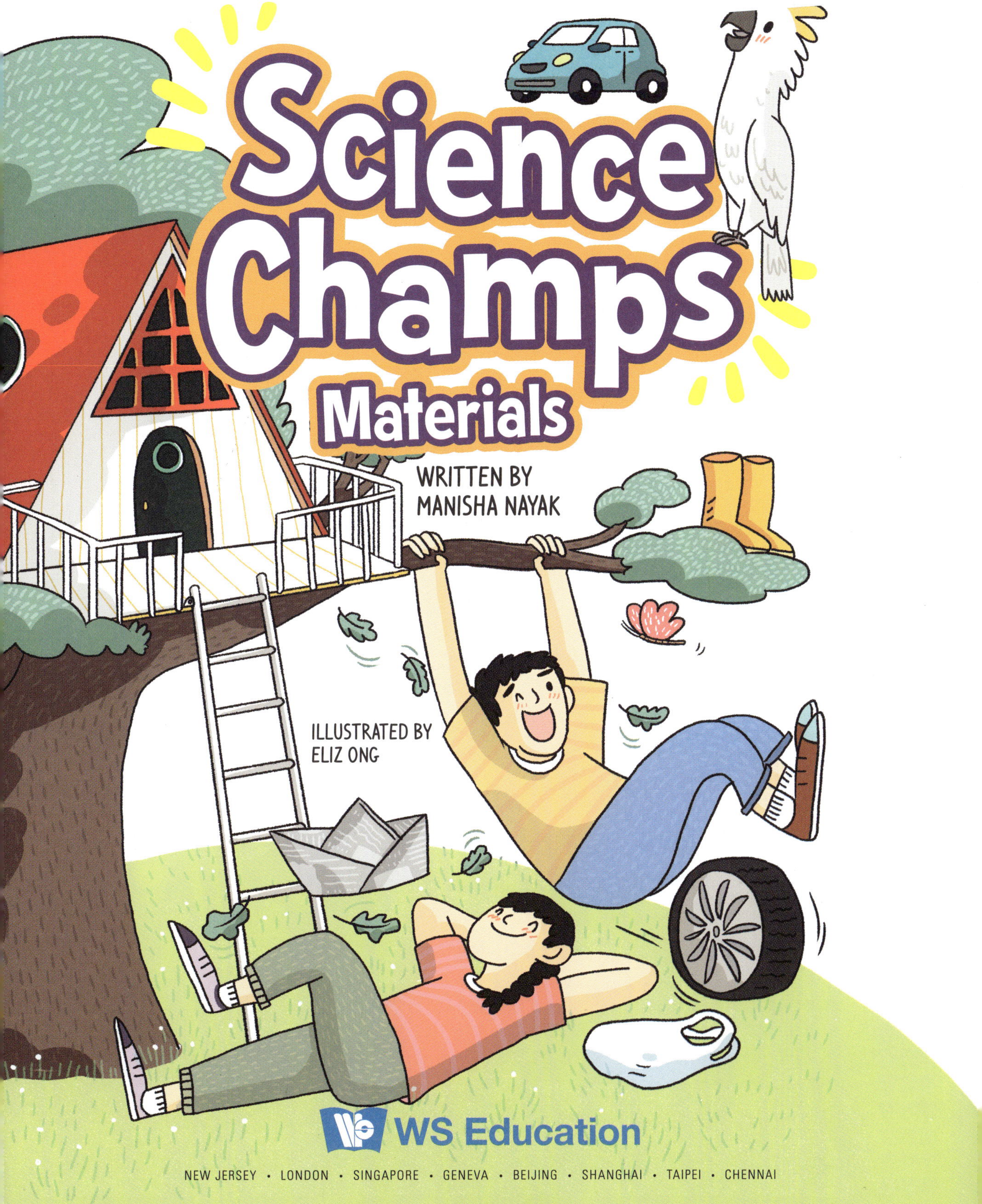

WS Education

NEW JERSEY • LONDON • SINGAPORE • GENEVA • BEIJING • SHANGHAI • TAIPEI • CHENNAI

Published by
WS Education, an imprint of
World Scientific Publishing Co. Pte. Ltd.
5 Toh Tuck Link, Singapore 596224
USA office: 27 Warren Street, Suite 401-402, Hackensack, NJ 07601
UK office: 57 Shelton Street, Covent Garden, London WC2H 9HE

National Library Board, Singapore Cataloguing in Publication Data

Name(s): Nayak, Manisha. | Ong, Eliz, illustrator.
Title: Materials / written by Manisha Nayak ; illustrated by Eliz Ong.
Other Title(s): Science champs.
Description: Singapore : WS Education, [2025]
Identifier(s): ISBN 978-981-12-9683-3 (hardcover) | 978-981-12-9684-0 (paperback) | 978-981-12-9685-7 (ebook for institutions) | 978-981-12-9686-4 (ebook for individuals)
Subject(s): LCSH: Materials--Comic books, strips, etc. | Graphic novels.
Classification: DDC 741.595957--dc23

British Library Cataloguing-in-Publication Data
A catalogue record for this book is available from the British Library.

Science Champs
MATERIALS

ISBN 978-981-12-9683-3 (hardcover)
ISBN 978-981-12-9684-0 (paperback)
ISBN 978-981-12-9685-7 (ebook for institutions)
ISBN 978-981-12-9686-4 (ebook for individuals)

Desk Editor: Daniele Lee

Printed in Malaysia

INTRODUCTION

Things around you are made of different materials. Some examples are wood, metal, plastic, ceramic, glass and rubber.

Different materials have different properties such as strength, flexibility, the ability to absorb water and the ability to allow light to pass through. Materials are chosen to make objects based on their properties.

JOIN US ON AN EXCITING JOURNEY TO FIND OUT MORE ABOUT THE MAGNIFICENT WORLD OF MATERIALS!

CONTENTS

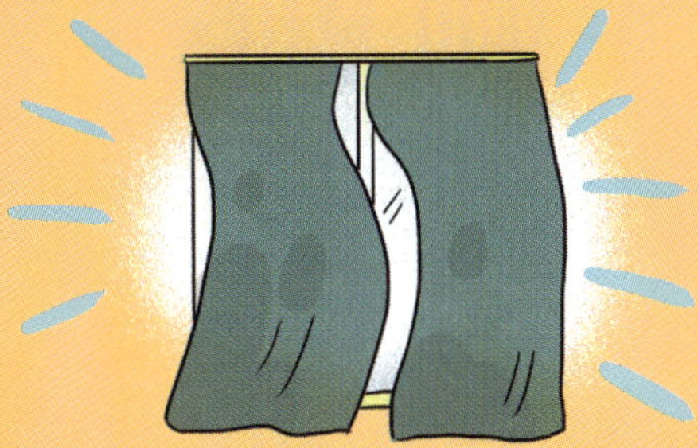

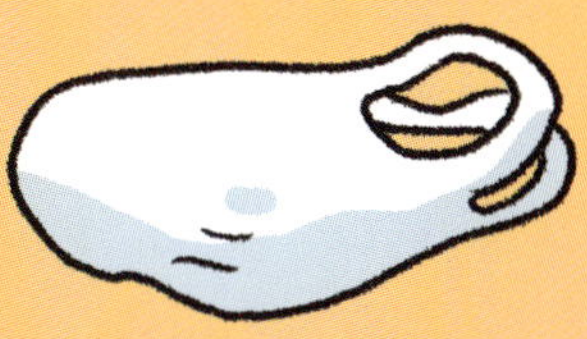

UNDER THE WEATHER

WE'LL MISS THE MATCH IF WE WAIT HERE FOR THE RAIN TO STOP. BUT IT'S RAINING SO HEAVILY!
MY HOME IS JUST 100 METRES AWAY. SHOULD WE MAKE A DASH FOR IT?
I DON'T HAVE AN UMBRELLA! I'LL GET COMPLETELY DRENCHED.
RENEE, I HAVE ONE. WE CAN SHARE IT.
ARE YOU SURE? IT'S QUITE SMALL. WE'LL BOTH GET HALF-WET!
BUT WE'LL BOTH BE HALF-DRY TOO!
OH, ZOYA, YOU'RE EVER THE OPTIMIST.

OKAY, WHAT ABOUT THE REST OF YOU?
WELL, I HAVE MY RAINCOAT.
WOW, YOU'RE WELL PREPARED, TIM!
I CAN HOLD THIS FOLDER OVER MY HEAD AND RUN.
WHAT ABOUT YOU, ALI?
I'LL JUST HOLD MY SCHOOLBAG OVER MY HEAD. LET'S GO!

HELLO, MR AND MRS RAHMAN. THANK YOU FOR HAVING US OVER.
I'M SORRY THAT I'VE TURNED UP LOOKING LIKE A WET HEDGEHOG.
WELL, I MUST SAY THE SPIKY HAIR LOOK SUITS YOU, ALI!
LET ME GET TOWELS FOR EVERYONE. AND A HAIR DRYER!
I DON'T THINK I'LL NEED A TOWEL.
WOW! LOOK, TIM IS COMPLETELY DRY.
ALL THANKS TO MY WATERPROOF RAINCOAT!

WATERPROOF...
OH YES, WE LEARNT ABOUT WATERPROOF MATERIALS IN CLASS LAST WEEK.
DID WE??
OH, ALI! WERE YOU DAYDREAMING IN CLASS AGAIN?
WATERPROOF MATERIALS ARE MATERIALS THAT DON'T ALLOW WATER TO PASS THROUGH THEM. THEY HELP KEEP THINGS DRY.
LET ME SEE. TIM, YOUR RAINCOAT IS MADE OF RUBBER, WHICH IS A WATERPROOF MATERIAL. THAT'S WHY YOU MANAGED TO STAY DRY!
dry
MY FOLDER IS MADE OF PLASTIC, WHICH IS WATERPROOF TOO. SO, MY HEAD, WHICH WAS UNDER THE FOLDER, IS DRY.
wet

MY UMBRELLA IS ALSO MADE OF A WATERPROOF MATERIAL. THAT HELPED RENEE AND ME TO STAY DRY.
wet
wet
WELL, NOT COMPLETELY DRY, BUT HALF EACH, AT LEAST.
WHOLE!
YOU KNOW WHAT THEY SAY! TWO HALVES MAKE A WHOLE!
WELL, MY BAG DOESN'T SEEM TO HAVE DONE ANYTHING TO HELP ME!
WELL, MR WET HEDGEHOG, YOUR BAG IS MADE OF FABRIC. IT'S NOT WATERPROOF.
SO THE RAINWATER WENT RIGHT THROUGH.

ALL ABOUT WATER
SCIENCE
WAIT, IF THE RAINWATER WENT RIGHT THROUGH, I WONDER WHAT'S HAPPENED TO MY BOOKS!
OH GOSH! OPEN YOUR BAG, QUICK!
OH NO! THIS IS MY HOMEWORK. THE PAGES ARE WET AND STUCK TOGETHER!
ALI
ALI
WELL, I HAVE THE PERFECT SOLUTION.
ZOYA, YOU ARE BRILLIANT!
ALI

THE END

INSPIRED BY NATURE

Waterproof materials are very useful in our daily lives. They are used to make many things, from raincoats and shoes to watches and mobile phones. Scientists are constantly working to make better and better waterproof materials.

Some waterproof materials have been developed that actively repel water! Did you know that many such materials developed have been inspired by nature? This is known as biomimicry.

Take the lotus plant, for example. You may have seen lotus plants in ponds, with their brightly coloured flowers and large floating leaves.

A lotus flower and leaves in a pond

If you take a closer look at the leaves of a lotus plant, especially after it has rained, you will notice that the leaves do not seem to get wet. Instead, the raindrops simply roll away from the leaf surface.

This property of repelling water is very important for the survival of the lotus plant. Lotus leaves have large and broad floating leaves so they can get enough sunlight to make food. If the leaves absorbed water, they would become too heavy and sink. If they sank, they would not get enough sunlight to make food for the plant. As a result, the plant would die.

Scientists have studied the lotus leaf in great detail to understand the properties that help it to remain dry. They have found that the tiny bumps on the leaf, as well as a waxy coating, are the main reasons why lotus leaves are able to repel water. Using their findings, scientists have been able to design materials that can stay dry even underwater! Can you think of some uses for such materials?

TAKE THE CHALLENGE!

What is another word for 'water-repelling'?

- Hydrophilic
- Hydropower
- Hydroponics
- Hydrophobic

ANSWER: HYDROPHOBIC

REMARKABLE RUBBER

HI EVERYONE! MY NAME IS REX, AND I'LL BE SHOWING YOU AROUND THE RUBBER PLANTATION. EVER BEEN TO ONE BEFORE?
NEVER! I DIDN'T EVEN KNOW RUBBER CAME FROM TREES. I THOUGHT IT WAS MADE IN FACTORIES.
WELL, YOU'RE NOT ENTIRELY WRONG. THERE ARE DIFFERENT TYPES OF RUBBER. SYNTHETIC RUBBER IS INDEED MADE IN FACTORIES.
BUT NATURAL RUBBER COMES FROM TREES. JUST LIKE THE ONES YOU SEE AROUND YOU!
WOW, HOW TALL ARE THESE TREES?
THE TREES IN PLANTATIONS GROW ABOUT 25 METRES TALL. IN THE WILD, THEY CAN GROW TO ABOUT 40 METRES!

LOOK! WHAT IS THAT?
THIS IS THE FRUIT OF THE RUBBER TREE.
OH, IS THAT WHERE RUBBER COMES FROM?
NO, RUBBER IS NOT MADE FROM THE FRUITS, BUT FROM ANOTHER PART OF THE TREE. CAN YOU GUESS WHICH PART?
THE LEAVES?
THE SEEDS?
THE ROOTS?
THE FLOWERS?
NOPE.

NATURAL RUBBER IS ACTUALLY MADE FROM THE LATEX OF RUBBER TREES.
LATEX? WHAT IS THAT?
LATEX IS A MILKY FLUID PRODUCED BY RUBBER TREES.
THE FIRST STEP IN MAKING RUBBER IS TO COLLECT LATEX FROM THE TREES.
A CUT IS MADE IN THE BARK OF THE TREE, WHICH MAKES THE LATEX OOZE OUT.
THIS LOOKS LIKE MILK! WHAT IS IT MADE OF?
AND WHY EXACTLY DO THESE TREES PRODUCE LATEX?

EXCELLENT QUESTIONS. LATEX IS A COMPLEX MIXTURE CONTAINING MANY SUBSTANCES.
TREES PRODUCE LATEX TO PROTECT THEMSELVES FROM GERMS AND INSECTS WHEN THEY ARE INJURED.
HELP!
OH! SO, DOES THE TREE DIE AFTER THE LATEX IS COLLECTED?
NO. AS YOU CAN SEE, WE DO NOT CUT DOWN THE TREES TO COLLECT THE LATEX.
THE CUTS IN THE TRUNKS ARE MADE BY SKILLED WORKERS USING PRECISE TOOLS.
IF LATEX COLLECTION IS PROPERLY MANAGED, A TREE CAN SURVIVE AND CONTINUE TO GIVE LATEX FOR MANY YEARS.

THE LATEX DRIPS INTO THESE SMALL BUCKETS THAT HAVE BEEN ATTACHED TO THE TREES.
THIS PROCESS OF COLLECTING LATEX IS CALLED RUBBER TAPPING. MULTIPLE TREES ARE TAPPED TO COLLECT ENOUGH LATEX.
HOW IS LATEX MADE INTO RUBBER?
RUBBER BAND
THE LATEX HAS TO UNDERGO SEVERAL STEPS BEFORE WE CAN GET RUBBER.
THE LATEX IS TAKEN TO A PROCESSING PLANT WHERE CHEMICALS ARE USED TO COAGULATE OR THICKEN THE LATEX TO EXTRACT RAW SHEETS OF RUBBER.
CHEMICALS ADDED
LATEX
THE RUBBER SHEETS ARE RUN THROUGH HEAVY ROLLERS TO REMOVE EXCESS WATER.

THE SHEETS OF RUBBER ARE THEN CUT AND STACKED TO BE SENT OFF TO OTHER PROCESSING PLANTS TO BE MADE INTO RUBBER PRODUCTS.
AND THAT IS HOW THIS TYRE WAS MADE! FASCINATING...
AND THESE BOOTS TOO!
I'LL NEVER LOOK AT CAR TYRES, BOOTS, ERASERS OR RUBBER BANDS THE SAME WAY AGAIN!
THANK YOU FOR THE TOUR, REX. THIS WAS VERY INTERESTING.
YOU'RE VERY WELCOME. GIVE US A CALL IF YOU'D LIKE TO VISIT AGAIN!
OR WE'LL SEND YOU A LA-TEX MESSAGE!
HAHAHA!
THE END

WAXY WONDER

Ever wondered what gives some candies their hard, glossy coating?

The answer is wax! Carnauba wax is a special type of wax that is used to make candies hard and glossy. The hard, waxy coating also ensures that the candies melt only in your mouth and not in your hand!

So where does carnauba wax come from?

Carnauba wax is a natural material that comes from the leaves of the carnauba palm, a plant found only in Brazil. The wax is obtained by collecting the leaves, drying them and beating them to loosen the wax. The wax flakes are then collected and processed before the wax is used.

Carnauba wax is extracted from the leaves of the carnauba palm.

As carnauba wax is non-toxic and safe for consumption, it is suitable for many uses in the food industry. It is used as a coating for candies, fruits, nuts, some cheeses and many other food items. If you have wondered why some apples appear so glossy, carnauba wax is the answer!

Apples are coated with a thin layer of wax to prevent moisture loss and keep them fresh for longer.

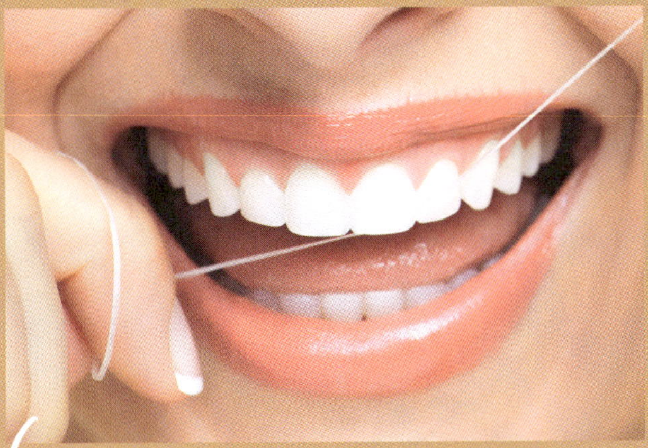

Carnauba wax is even used in dental floss! It helps the floss glide smoothly between teeth.

In addition, carnauba wax is used to make cosmetics such as lipstick, eyeliners, foundation and deodorant. It is also used to coat medicinal pills to make them easier to swallow. The shiny, protective coating of some vehicles is also due to a layer of carnauba wax.

TAKE THE CHALLENGE!

Beeswax is another type of natural wax. It is extracted from ________.

- honey
- pollen
- beehives
- honeybees

ANSWER: BEEHIVES

A POTTERY WORKSHOP

HAHA!
NO, TYLA, NOT A POETRY WORKSHOP. A POTTERY WORKSHOP!
WHAT IS A POTTERY WORKSHOP?
WELL, HOW WOULD YOU LIKE TO SPEND TOMORROW AFTERNOON MAKING CERAMIC POTS ON A POTTER'S WHEEL?
AN ACTUAL POTTER'S WHEEL? I'VE ONLY SEEN IT IN BOOKS!
YES!
THAT SOUNDS SO EXCITING!
YES, BUT BE PREPARED TO GET YOUR HANDS ALL BROWN AND MUDDY!
I DON'T MIND AT ALL!

THE NEXT DAY...
WELCOME TO TODAY'S POTTERY WORKSHOP! I'M JEAN, YOUR INSTRUCTOR. WHO'S LOOKING FORWARD TO MAKING SOME FUN CERAMIC ITEMS?
ME!
ME!
ME! WHAT ARE WE MAKING TODAY?
OH, ABSOLUTELY ANYTHING YOU WANT. LET YOUR IMAGINATION FLY!
IF YOU NEED SOME IDEAS, HERE ARE SOME CREATIONS BY OTHER KIDS. YOU COULD MAKE A VASE, A MUG OR A SOUP BOWL. OR ANYTHING ELSE YOU WANT!
I THINK I'LL MAKE A VASE TO KEEP FLOWERS IN. WHAT ABOUT YOU, TYLA?
HMMM... I HAVEN'T DECIDED YET. LET ME THINK...

ALL RIGHT, POTTERS! LET'S GET STARTED.
WHAT IS THIS?
THIS IS CLAY. MAKING CERAMIC ITEMS STARTS WITH SHAPING THE CLAY.
POKE POKE
THE CLAY IS SO SOFT. BUT CERAMIC ITEMS ARE SO HARD.
GOOD OBSERVATION, TINA! THERE ARE SEVERAL STEPS THAT CHANGE THIS SOFT LUMP OF CLAY INTO A HARD CERAMIC ITEM.
FIRST, WE USE THE POTTER'S WHEEL TO SHAPE THE CLAY. THE SPINNING WHEEL HELPS US TO SHAPE THE CLAY EVENLY ALL AROUND.

OOOH, THE CLAY FEELS SO COOL AND SMOOTH.
YES, I FIND THIS VERY RELAXING.
15 MINUTES LATER...
I THINK I'M DONE!
WOW, THAT LOOKS GREAT!
MY VASE IS STILL WET AND SOFT THOUGH. IF I TRY TO TAKE IT OFF THE WHEEL, I'M SURE I'LL SQUASH IT!
YOU'RE RIGHT, TINA. WE USE THIS SPECIAL WIRE TO UNSTICK THE BASE AND GENTLY TAKE IT OFF THE WHEEL.
WOW, YOU MANAGED TO REMOVE IT WITHOUT SQUASHING IT!
THAT'S THE RESULT OF LOTS OF PRACTICE!
WHAT'S NEXT?
WE WILL DRY IT AND THEN BAKE IT IN A SPECIAL OVEN.

BAKE IT? LIKE HOW WE BAKE COOKIES?
HAHA! WELL, KIND OF. JUST LIKE HOW SOFT COOKIE DOUGH TURNS TO HARD AND CRUNCHY COOKIES DURING BAKING, THIS VASE WILL ALSO HARDEN AND BECOME STRONGER AFTER BAKING.
DRY
BAKE
WE WILL DRY AND BAKE YOUR CREATIONS FOR YOU. YOU CAN COME BACK NEXT WEEK TO PAINT THEM!
THAT SOUNDS EXCITING!
WOW, LOOK AT MY HANDS. LET ME GO WASH THEM.
TINA, BEFORE YOU WASH YOUR HANDS, COULD YOU PLEASE HELP ME SHAPE MY BOWL PROPERLY? IT'S A LITTLE LOPSIDED.
OF COURSE, TYLA!

NEXT WEEK...
MUM, WE ARE BACK WITH OUR COMPLETED CERAMIC CREATIONS!
BE CAREFUL. CERAMIC IS A HARD AND STRONG MATERIAL, BUT IT ALSO BREAKS VERY EASILY IF DROPPED.
WOW!
THAT IS BEAUTIFUL, TINA!
LOOK AT MINE! LOOK AT MINE!
WHAT A NICE BOWL!
OH DEAR. IT LOOKS LIKE I CAN'T USE IT.
WHY NOT?
BECAUSE... IT'S FOR BUBBLES!
WOOF!
BUBBLES
I THINK BUBBLES IS SAYING, 'THANK YOU, TYLA!'

THE END

SUPER CERAMIC

We usually associate ceramic with cooking utensils such as plates, bowls and spoons. Ceramic is also commonly used to make vases and flowerpots. However, this fascinating material also makes an appearance in some unusual places where you may not have noticed it!

Ceramics are used to make bricks. These bricks are used to construct houses and buildings.

Many people keep small ceramic plant pots in the bathroom. However, that's not the only place in the bathroom where you'll find ceramic. Did you know that most toilet bowls are also made of ceramic?

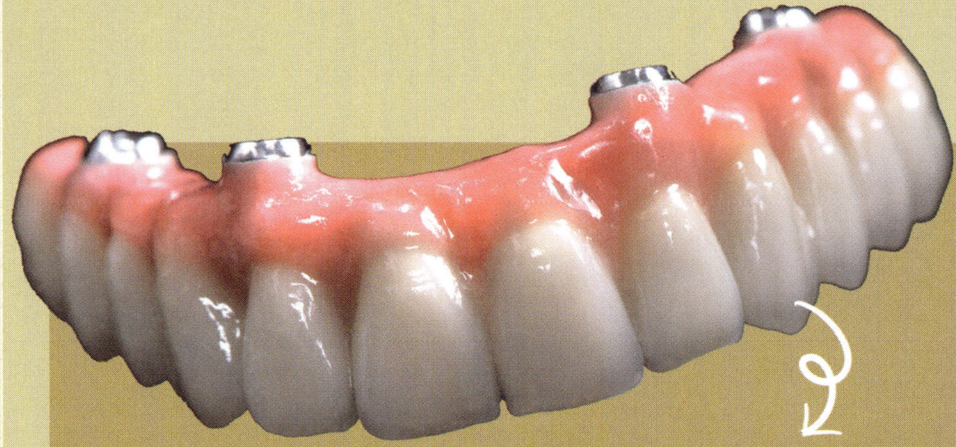

Some ceramics can even be found in the human body! For example, ceramic is used to make man-made teeth.

TAKE THE CHALLENGE!

The oven used to bake clay pottery to harden it into ceramic is called a ____________.

- kiln
- grill
- barbecue
- incinerator

ANSWER: KILN

CURTAIN CALL
OH, SOMEBODY LOOKS GRUMPY TODAY. WHAT HAPPENED, LITTLE BRO?
I THINK RON DIDN'T HAVE A GOOD NAP. SOMETHING MUST HAVE DISTURBED HIM.
WAAA!
HEY, DON'T BLAME ME!
I MAY BE THE LOUDEST THING IN THIS HOUSE, BUT I'M ALWAYS VERY QUIET DURING RON'S NAPS.
I THINK IT'S THE CURTAINS IN RON'S ROOM.
WHAT'S WRONG WITH THE CURTAINS?
THEY DON'T KEEP THE ROOM FULLY DARK. SO, RON KEEPS WAKING UP DURING HIS AFTERNOON NAPS.

AND WE ALL KNOW HOW IMPORTANT THESE NAPS ARE FOR TIRED TODDLERS!
DON'T WORRY, MUM. WE'LL FIND A SOLUTION.
WE NEED BLACKOUT CURTAINS.
WHAT ARE BLACKOUT CURTAINS? CURTAINS THAT CAUSE A BLACKOUT??
BLACKOUT! BLACKOUT!
HAHA! NO, RAJ. BLACKOUT CURTAINS HELP TO KEEP A ROOM FULLY DARK, EVEN DURING THE DAY!
FULLY DARK? DURING THE DAY? HOW??

TO UNDERSTAND, YOU NEED TO KNOW ABOUT THE TRANSPARENCY OF MATERIALS FIRST.
GLASS
LIGHT
THESE WINDOWPANES ARE MADE OF GLASS. GLASS IS A TRANSPARENT MATERIAL. THIS MEANS THAT IT ALLOWS MOST LIGHT TO PASS THROUGH.
NOW IMAGINE IF WE DIDN'T HAVE ANY CURTAINS. HOW WOULD THE ROOM BE IN THE AFTERNOONS?
OH. VERY, VERY BRIGHT!
JUST LIKE ME!
NOW TAKE A LOOK AT THESE CURTAINS. THEY ARE TRANSLUCENT. THIS MEANS THAT THEY ALLOW SOME LIGHT TO PASS THROUGH THEM.

WHEN I CLOSE THE CURTAINS, THE ROOM IS NOT AS BRIGHT AS BEFORE, BUT SOME LIGHT IS STILL ENTERING THE ROOM.
SO THE ROOM IS NOT COMPLETELY DARK. AND THAT DISTURBS RON'S AFTERNOON NAP.
THE TRANSLUCENT CURTAINS ARE NOT ABLE TO BLOCK ENOUGH LIGHT TO MAKE THE ROOM COMPLETELY DARK.
YES.
WE NEED AN OPAQUE MATERIAL.
WHAT'S AN OPAQUE MATERIAL?
AN OPAQUE MATERIAL DOES NOT ALLOW LIGHT TO PASS THROUGH IT.

BLACKOUT CURTAINS ARE OPAQUE. WHEN CLOSED, THEY CAN MAKE THE ROOM AS DARK AS NIGHT!
WOW! HOW DO THEY DO THAT?
WITH BLACKOUT CURTAINS, RON'S ROOM CAN BE FULLY DARK EVEN DURING THE AFTERNOONS!
THEY HAVE A LINING MADE OF A TIGHTLY-WOVEN MATERIAL THAT CAN BLOCK OUT LIGHT.
TOMORROW IS A SATURDAY. LET'S GET THE BLACKOUT CURTAINS TOMORROW.
SOUNDS LIKE A PLAN. RAJ, WOULD YOU PLEASE BABYSIT RON WHILE WE'RE OUT?
OF COURSE!
AND I'LL ASSIST!

THE NEXT AFTERNOON...
SORRY, RAJ, WE GOT DELAYED AT THE CURTAIN SHOP.
SHHH...
WHAT HAPPENED??
RON IS NAPPING PEACEFULLY. IN A VERY DARK ROOM.
A VERY DARK ROOM? WHAT DO YOU MEAN?
!?
WELL, I CREATED MY OWN HOMEMADE TEMPORARY BLACKOUT SCREEN. COME, LOOK!

WOW! HOW DID YOU MAKE THE ROOM SO DARK?
SIMPLE. I TAPED PIECES OF CARDBOARD OVER THE GLASS WINDOWS!
PAMPAM
THAT'S SO CLEVER, RAJ!
IT WAS MY IDEA.
WELL, I NEEDED SOMETHING OPAQUE! I KNOW IT LOOKS UGLY, BUT I FIGURED IT WOULD DO TILL YOU GOT HOME WITH THE BLACKOUT CURTAINS.
AWW, LOOK AT RON, SLEEPING SO SOUNDLY.
SHHHHH!
THE END

SEE-THROUGH ANIMALS

Many objects we use in our daily lives are transparent. We can see through windowpanes and the lenses of glasses. However, did you know that nature also has some amazing 'see-through' creatures? This mind-blowing feature makes them harder to spot and protects them from being hunted and eaten by other animals. Let's look at some cool examples!

Glass shrimp

Glasswing butterfly

Glass frog

Amazon crystal tetra

TAKE THE CHALLENGE!

This transparent living thing is a _________.

- squid
- octopus
- seahorse
- sea jelly (jellyfish)

ANSWER: SEA JELLY (JELLYFISH)

THE TERRIFIC TREEHOUSE

WE ARE BUILDING A TREEHOUSE!
A WHAAAAT??
A TREEHOUSE. A HOUSE IN THE TREE. COME UP AND SEE! THERE'S A LADDER.
BE CAREFUL, NUR.
HELLO!
NUR, THIS IS ALEX. HE IS HELPING ME BUILD THE TREEHOUSE.
GRANDMA, YOU MEAN THERE WILL BE A HOUSE IN THIS TREE?
YES! A SMALL ONE.

THAT SOUNDS SO EXCITING! A HOUSE UP IN A TREE!
WHAT WOULD IT BE MADE OF?
MAINLY WOOD. AND SOME OTHER MATERIALS.
A WOODEN HOUSE? IT WON'T BREAK, WILL IT?
NO, NUR. WOOD IS AN EXCELLENT BUILDING MATERIAL. IT'S WIDELY USED TO MAKE THINGS LIKE HOUSES, BOATS AND FURNITURE.
TO MAKE A HOUSE UP ON A TREE, WE NEED TO CHOOSE THE MATERIAL CAREFULLY.
A TREEHOUSE NEEDS TO BE MADE OF A MATERIAL THAT IS NOT TOO HEAVY.
AT THE SAME TIME, IT NEEDS TO BE STRONG SO IT CAN SUPPORT THE WEIGHT OF PEOPLE.

WOOD IS PERFECT FOR THIS. IT'S NOT AS HEAVY AS METAL OR CONCRETE, BUT IT'S STRONG AND RIGID.
WOOD CAN ALSO BE EASILY CUT INTO DIFFERENT SHAPES TO MAKE DIFFERENT PARTS OF THE TREEHOUSE.
IN FACT, MOST TREEHOUSES ARE MADE OF WOOD.
WOULD THE ENTIRE TREEHOUSE BE MADE OF WOOD?
NO, WE'LL USE OTHER MATERIALS TOO. FOR EXAMPLE, THE NAILS TO CONNECT THE PIECES OF WOOD ARE MADE OF METAL. SOME PARTS OF THE TREEHOUSE WILL ALSO BE MADE OF PLASTIC.
IT SOUNDS SO EXCITING. WHEN WILL THE TREEHOUSE BE READY?
WELL, COME BY IN A WEEK!
WOW!
I CAN'T WAIT TO SEE THE COMPLETED TREEHOUSE!

NEXT WEEK...
SO... WHAT DO YOU THINK, NUR?
LET'S SEE... MIND-BLOWING?
GRANDMA, I HAVE... NO WORDS. THIS IS JUST...
YES!
WELL, WHAT ARE WE WAITING FOR? LET'S GO UP AND CHECK IT OUT!

HELLO, ALEX. THIS PLACE LOOKS AMAZING. IT'S STRAIGHT OUT OF A STORYBOOK!
IT DOES! THANKS, ALEX. I'M SO GRATEFUL FOR THE EFFORT YOU'VE PUT INTO THE DESIGN AND SAFETY OF THE TREEHOUSE.
OH, WHAT'S THIS? A HAMMOCK?
YES, YOUR GRANDMA SPECIFICALLY WANTED ONE HERE.
CAN I HOP ON? WILL IT BREAK?
DON'T WORRY, IT'S VERY SAFE. IT'S MADE OF A STRONG AND FLEXIBLE FABRIC.
JUST WHEN I THOUGHT THE TREEHOUSE COULDN'T GET MORE AWESOME... I'M IN A HAMMOCK IN A TREEHOUSE!
GRANDMA, I MAY NEVER LEAVE THIS PLACE!
HAHA!

BUT GRANDMA, WHAT WOULD YOU DO IN THIS TREEHOUSE?
OH, I'D READ BOOKS AND DO SOME BIRD-WATCHING. OR JUST HAVE A PICNIC WITH THE OWNER.
THE OWNER?? AREN'T YOU THE OWNER? WHO'S THE OWNER OF THIS TREEHOUSE?
AH, JUST THIS ADVENTUROUS LITTLE GIRL WHO LIKES TO HANG OUT WITH HER OLD GRANDMA.
ME?? I'M THE OWNER OF THE TREEHOUSE??
YES, INDEED.
OH, GRANDMA! THANK YOU, THANK YOU, THANK YOU!

THE END

THE TREE OF LIFE

Trees are incredibly useful to humans. They provide us with many materials such as wood, rubber and paper. One tree in particular has so many uses that it has been nicknamed 'the tree of life'.

The African baobab tree is typically found in hot, dry regions of Africa. It is difficult for many plants to survive there, but the African baobab tree is very well adapted to its environment. The tree has a broad trunk, often made up of multiple stems fused together. The tree stores water in its trunk during the rainy season, which allows it to survive the dry season.

Baobab trees can live very long. In fact, scientists have found some baobab trees that are thousands of years old!

The baobab tree is a valued source of food, water and shelter for humans and other animals that live in the area. In fact, every part of the tree is believed to be useful. The bark is used to make rope, mats, baskets and even clothing. The fruit, which is very nutritious, can be eaten by itself or made into drinks and jams. The seeds are roasted to make a coffee-like substance or pressed to make oil for cooking and cosmetics. Even its leaves, flowers and roots can be eaten!

The fruit of the baobab tree is an important source of food.

The pollen of the flowers can be made into glue.

The African baobab is a resilient symbol of life in an environment where very little can survive. It truly lives up to its nickname 'the tree of life'.

TAKE THE CHALLENGE!

The baobab tree is also known as the 'upside-down tree' because ________________.

- [ ] its fruits hang upside down
- [ ] its branches grow under the soil
- [ ] its roots grow above the ground
- [ ] its branches look like upside-down roots

ANSWER: ITS BRANCHES LOOK LIKE UPSIDE-DOWN ROOTS

A CLEAN GETAWAY

HMM...
WHAT'S UP, ELLA? YOU SEEM LOST IN THOUGHT.
WE ARE LEARNING ABOUT MATERIALS IN SCHOOL THIS WEEK. OUR TEACHER ASKED US TO LOOK OUT FOR THINGS AROUND US THAT ARE MADE OF DIFFERENT MATERIALS.
SHE'S GOING TO QUIZ US NEXT WEEK. I'VE BEEN LOOKING FOR SUITABLE OBJECTS TO REVISE FOR THE QUIZ.
I JUST REALISED OUR CAR IS A PERFECT EXAMPLE OF AN OBJECT MADE OF DIFFERENT MATERIALS!
IT IS, INDEED. EVERY PART OF THE CAR HAS A SPECIFIC FUNCTION. THE MATERIAL CHOSEN TO MAKE AN OBJECT MUST BE SUITABLE FOR THE USE OF THE OBJECT.

ELLA, LET'S MAKE THIS FUN! CAN YOU POINT OUT FOUR DIFFERENT MATERIALS THAT HAVE BEEN USED TO MAKE THE CAR?
OOH! LIKE A TREASURE HUNT!
THE BODY OF THE CAR IS MADE OF METAL.
CORRECT. AND WHY IS METAL A SUITABLE CHOICE FOR IT?
METAL IS HARD AND STRONG, AND DOES NOT BREAK EASILY WHEN HIT. THE CAR'S METAL BODY PROTECTS THE DRIVER AND PASSENGERS.
METAL IS ALSO WATERPROOF. SO, IT DOES NOT ALLOW RAINWATER TO ENTER THE CAR!
GREAT JOB, ELLA!

OOH, I SPOTTED ANOTHER MATERIAL! THE WINDSCREEN IS MADE OF GLASS.
CORRECT. AND WHAT IMPORTANT PROPERTY OF GLASS MAKES IT SUITABLE TO MAKE A WINDSCREEN?
GLASS IS TRANSPARENT! IF THE WINDSCREEN WAS MADE OF ANOTHER MATERIAL, SUCH AS WOOD OR METAL, DRIVERS WOULD NOT BE ABLE TO SEE WHERE THEY WERE GOING!
CRASH!!
OH DEAR, THAT WOULD BE DISASTROUS INDEED!
GLASS
THE WINDSCREEN NEEDS TO BE STRONG FOR PROTECTION FROM WIND AND RAIN.
IT ALSO NEEDS TO BE WATERPROOF, OTHERWISE EVERYONE IN THE CAR WOULD GET DRENCHED WHEN IT RAINED!

OH, I FOUND ANOTHER MATERIAL. THE TYRES ARE MADE OF RUBBER!
AND WHY IS THAT?
THE TYRES ARE FOUND UNDER THE BODY OF THE CAR. SO THEY NEED TO BE ABLE TO SUPPORT THE HEAVY CAR.
YOU'RE RIGHT. OUR CAR WEIGHS MORE THAN 1000 KG. THE TYRES NEED TO BE MADE OF A STRONG MATERIAL THAT CAN SUPPORT THE WEIGHT OF THE CAR.
OTHERWISE THEY'D BE TOO TYRE-D!
HMM... I HAVE A QUESTION. METAL IS ALSO A STRONG MATERIAL. WHY AREN'T THE TYRES MADE OF METAL?
THAT'S A GREAT QUESTION, ELLA. OFTEN, MULTIPLE PROPERTIES OF A MATERIAL NEED TO BE CONSIDERED BEFORE IT'S CHOSEN TO MAKE SOMETHING.
METAL IS STIFF, UNLIKE RUBBER. RUBBER IS FLEXIBLE, WHICH ALLOWS THE CAR TO GO OVER ROUGH ROADS AND HUMPS WITHOUT CAUSING DISCOMFORT TO THE PEOPLE IN THE CAR.

ELLA, DO YOU WANT TO GET INSIDE THE CAR? YOU MAY FIND SOMETHING THERE!
OKAY, I THINK I'M ALL OUT OF MATERIALS!
OOH, THE CAR SEATS! THEY'RE COVERED IN FABRIC!
WELL DONE!
AND FABRIC WAS CHOSEN AS IT'S FLEXIBLE AND MAKES THE CAR SEATS COMFORTABLE TO SIT ON!
THAT'S RIGHT. LEATHER OR FABRIC ARE POPULAR CHOICES TO MAKE CAR SEATS AS THEY ARE FLEXIBLE.
SOME PEOPLE, ESPECIALLY THOSE WITH YOUNG CHILDREN, USE CAR SEATS THAT ARE COVERED WITH A WATERPROOF MATERIAL TO AVOID STAINS.

WOW, LOOK AT OUR SPARKLING CAR.
IT LOOKS BRAND NEW!
WE CLEANED IT IN RECORD TIME! THANKS FOR HELPING, ELLA.
THIS WAS SO MUCH FUN, DAD AND MUM! I REALLY ENJOYED IT. AND THE 'REVISION' ON MATERIALS TOO.
IT'S AMAZING HOW MANY MATERIALS CAN BE FOUND ALL AROUND US. SOMETIMES WE DON'T EVEN REALISE IT.
I THINK I'M FULLY READY TO ACE THE CLASS QUIZ ON MATERIALS!
THE END

MAGICAL MICROFIBRE

You may have used microfibre cloth for cleaning a variety of things such as mirrors, glass items and even your computer screen. Microfibre cloth is also commonly used to polish surfaces such as the body of a car without leaving behind any dust or streaks.

What is it about microfibre that makes it so suitable to clean these items?

Unlike cotton and wool, microfibre is a synthetic fabric made of materials such as nylon and polyester. Its name comes from the fact that it is made of very fine fibres. In the best-quality microfibre fabric, these fibres can be 200 times thinner than a human hair! The fine fibres increase the surface area of the microfibre cloth, allowing it to trap more dirt than regular cleaning cloths. The microfibres are also shredded along their sides, creating more slots to trap dirt and prevent it from falling out.

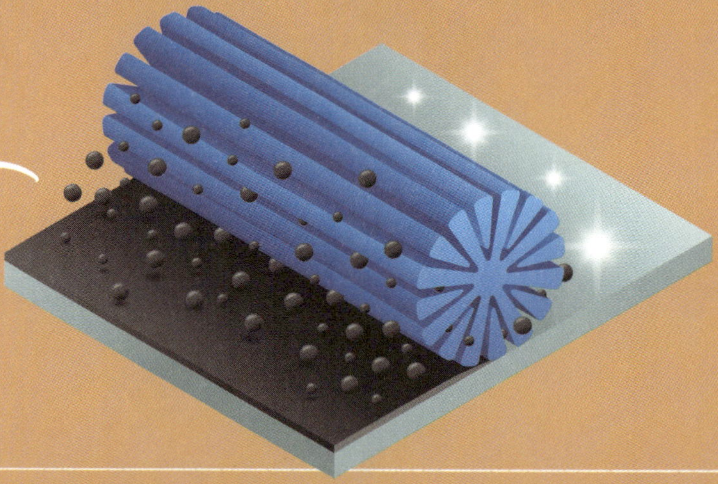

The special structure of microfibre allows it to remove dirt from a surface efficiently.

The shredding also makes microfibre great at both absorbing water and releasing the absorbed water efficiently. No wonder it's easier and faster to wring out and dry a microfibre cloth compared to a cotton cloth. This property makes microfibre ideal for making mops and towels too.

Microfibre mops absorb water efficiently.

Microfibre fabric has been designed to attract dust, so cleaning surfaces requires less effort, with almost no residue left behind after only a few wipes.

Smooth surfaces such as phones are often cleaned with microfibre to achieve a spotless and shiny surface with no streaks.

TAKE THE CHALLENGE!

Microfibre is made of materials such as nylon and polyester. Nylon and polyester are usually made from ________.

- [ ] coal
- [ ] rubber
- [ ] beeswax
- [ ] petroleum

ANSWER: PETROLEUM

MAKE IT FLOAT!

OH LOOK, HERE'S THE CAPTAIN OF OUR BOAT.
WELL, HE LOOKS DETERMINED. LET'S NAME HIM CAPTAIN UNSINKABLE!
THAT'S A GOOD NAME! I LIKE IT.
WE HAVE COMPLETED THE CHAPTER ON MATERIALS AND THEIR PROPERTIES. I TRUST THAT YOU WILL PUT YOUR KNOWLEDGE TO GOOD USE.
OKAY, SO WHAT DO WE HAVE HERE? A TUB OF WATER, NEWSPAPER, ALUMINIUM FOIL, A PIECE OF WOOD, A PIECE OF STYROFOAM, A PLASTIC SHEET, A STEEL BOWL, RUBBER BANDS, GLUE, STRING, SCISSORS AND A STAPLER.
GLUE

I KNOW! LET'S MAKE A PAPER BOAT BY FOLDING THE NEWSPAPER!
OH, YES! GOOD IDEA. OUR ORIGAMI CHAMPION ALYA TO THE RESCUE!
ALL RIGHT, TIME TO TEST THE BOAT!
YAY! WE DID IT! IT'S FLOATING!
THE NEWSPAPER IS WET. THE BOAT IS SINKING!
OH DEAR...

LET'S TRY THE STEEL BOWL. IT'S WATERPROOF SO IT WON'T ABSORB WATER LIKE OUR NEWSPAPER BOAT DID.
OH NO, IT SANK RIGHT AWAY!
!!
LIFEGUARD SAM DIVING IN TO RESCUE CAPTAIN UNSINKABLE!
BOY, HE DOESN'T LOOK HAPPY.
OKAY, HOW ABOUT WE MAKE A RAFT USING A PIECE OF ALUMINIUM FOIL?
YES, ALUMINIUM IS ALSO A METAL LIKE STEEL, BUT THE FOIL IS THIN. I THINK IT WILL FLOAT!

OKAY, LET'S TRY THIS.
YES, IT FLOATS!
ALUMINIUM FOIL
BUT WE HAVEN'T PUT CAPTAIN UNSINKABLE ON IT YET!
HERE YOU GO, CAPTAIN. SAIL AWAY!
YIKES! MORE LIKE 'SINK AWAY'!
OH DEAR, CAPTAIN UNSINKABLE IS NOT REALLY LIVING UP TO HIS NAME, IS HE?

LET'S TRY THE PLASTIC SHEET? PLASTIC FLOATS ON WATER!
PLASTIC SHEET
IT'S TOO FLEXIBLE. IT FLOATS BUT IT CAN'T HOLD UP ANY WEIGHT ON IT.
YOU'RE RIGHT. WE NEED SOMETHING STIFF THAT CAPTAIN UNSINKABLE CAN STAND ON.
HMMM, HOW ABOUT THIS PIECE OF WOOD?
OH YES, LET'S TRY THE PIECE OF WOOD. MANY BOATS AND RAFTS ARE MADE OF WOOD!
IT'S HALF-FLOATING, BUT IT STARTS TO SINK WHEN I PLACE CAPTAIN UNSINKABLE ON IT.
YEAH, IT DOESN'T LOOK VERY STABLE. WE NEED TO IMPROVE IT.

LET'S TRY THE STYROFOAM PIECE. BET IT WILL FLOAT!
YES, IT FLOATS BUT IT'S TOO LIGHT. IT KEEPS TOPPLING OVER WHEN I PLACE CAPTAIN UNSINKABLE ON IT.
HEY, HOW ABOUT WE USE TWO MATERIALS? WE COULD ATTACH THE STYROFOAM PIECE UNDER THE PIECE OF WOOD!
BRILLIANT!
YES! IT WORKS!
PHEW! CAPTAIN UNSINKABLE IS FINALLY UNSINKABLE!
THE END

SHIP AHOY!

Have you ever wondered why a small metal coin sinks in water but a large metal ship floats?

To understand this, we need to first know what density of a material is. Density is the amount of mass per unit of volume. Different materials have different densities. For example, a steel ball is heavier than a wooden ball of the same size, because steel is denser than wood.

An object will float on water if its density is less than the density of water.

The stone sinks but the cork floats on water. This is because the stone is denser than water, but the cork is less dense than water.

A steel coin sinks in water because steel is denser than water. However, a steel ship, which is much larger and heavier than the coin, is able to float on water. How is that possible?

The secret to this is air! Think of an eraser and a rubber duck. Both are made of the same material, rubber. An eraser sinks in water, but a rubber duck is able to float because it has air inside. This lowers the average density of the rubber duck to less than that of water. If it was made of solid rubber without any air inside, it would sink like the eraser.

A rubber duck is able to float on water because it has air inside.

Similarly, the interior of a ship is hollow and contains a lot of air. This lowers the average density of the ship to less than that of water. Hence, the ship is able to float on water.

TAKE THE CHALLENGE!

These balloons rise in the air as they are filled with ________, which is less dense than air.

- [ ] water
- [ ] helium
- [ ] oxygen
- [ ] carbon dioxide

ANSWER: HELIUM

THE PLASTIC PROBLEM

PLEASE MAKE SURE YOU DON'T TOUCH ANY OF THE LITTER WITH YOUR BARE HANDS. IT CAN BE DANGEROUS. USE THE TONGS GIVEN TO YOU.
WE WILL PLACE THE LITTER WE COLLECT IN THESE BAGS.
OH, LOOK!
BALLOONS! LOOKS LIKE SOMEONE HAD A BIRTHDAY PARTY HERE.
AND THEY FORGOT TO CLEAN UP BEFORE THEY LEFT. THESE BALLOONS CAN EASILY GET BLOWN INTO THE WATER AND HARM THE ANIMALS.
ALL DONE!

OH DEAR,
WHAT HAPPENED?
AAAAH!
HE'S BLEEDING BADLY. WE NEED TO TAKE HIM TO THE DOCTOR NOW.
OH LOOK! A BROKEN BOTTLE!
THIS MUST HAVE CUT THE BOY'S FOOT WHEN HE WAS PLAYING IN THE SAND.
YES. LITTER THAT IS NOT DISPOSED OF PROPERLY CAN BE VERY DANGEROUS. PLEASE BE CAREFUL AS YOU WALK AROUND.

WOW, LOOK AT THIS BIG PILE OF LITTER. OLD TOOTHBRUSHES, BOTTLES, TOYS AND PLASTIC BAGS...
CAN ANYONE TELL ME WHAT IS COMMON AMONG THESE ITEMS?
THEY'RE ALL MADE OF PLASTIC!
THAT'S RIGHT. IN FACT, MOST OF THE LITTER FOUND IN BEACHES IS MADE UP OF PLASTIC PRODUCTS.
WHY IS PLASTIC USED TO MAKE SO MANY THINGS?
PLASTIC IS A POPULAR MATERIAL FOR MAKING MANY OBJECTS AS IT HAS MANY USEFUL PROPERTIES.
IT'S LIGHT, WATERPROOF, CHEAP AND CAN BE SHAPED EASILY INTO DIFFERENT THINGS.

HOWEVER, WHEN IT'S THROWN AWAY AS WASTE, PLASTIC IS HARMFUL FOR THE ENVIRONMENT. COMPARED TO OTHER WASTE SUCH AS VEGETABLE PEELS, PLASTICS TAKE AN EXTREMELY LONG TIME TO BREAK DOWN.
I READ SOMEWHERE THAT IT TAKES ABOUT 450 YEARS FOR A PLASTIC BOTTLE TO BREAK DOWN COMPLETELY.
YES, MANY PLASTICS CAN STAY IN THE ENVIRONMENT FOR HUNDREDS OF YEARS, CONTAMINATING THE SOIL AND WATER, AND CAUSING HARM TO LIVING THINGS.
THE WORST PART IS THAT MANY OF THESE ARE SINGLE-USE PLASTICS.
WHAT ARE SINGLE-USE PLASTICS?
?
chips
SINGLE-USE PLASTICS ARE PLASTIC PRODUCTS THAT WE ONLY USE ONCE BEFORE THROWING THEM AWAY. SOME EXAMPLES ARE FOOD CONTAINERS, STRAWS, PLASTIC BOTTLES AND FOOD WRAPPERS.

TWO HOURS LATER...
LOOK! THE BEACH LOOKS SO MUCH CLEANER!
CHECK OUT HOW MANY BAGS OF TRASH WE HAVE COLLECTED!
WELL DONE, STUDENTS!
WE HAVE DONE VERY WELL TODAY. HOWEVER, WE MUST REMEMBER THAT CLEANING UP THE BEACH IS JUST ONE STEP TOWARDS MAINTAINING A CLEAN ENVIRONMENT.
WE SHOULD NOT DIRTY IT IN THE FIRST PLACE!
YOU'RE RIGHT! THERE ARE MANY MORE THINGS WE CAN DO FOR THE ENVIRONMENT.
TOMORROW WHEN WE'RE BACK IN CLASS, WE'D LIKE EACH OF YOU TO SHARE IDEAS ON SIMPLE THINGS WE CAN DO TO MANAGE THE PROBLEM OF PLASTIC WASTE.

BUY VEGETABLES FROM VEGETABLE MARKETS INSTEAD OF SUPERMARKETS WHERE THEY ARE WRAPPED IN SINGLE-USE PLASTIC.
SOIL
SUPER MART
DO NOT USE PLASTIC STRAWS.
Reuse plastic objects.
Use reusable bags for shopping.
TAKE YOUR OWN CONTAINER TO PACK TAKEAWAY FOOD.
DISPOSE OF RECYCLABLE PLASTIC TRASH IN THE RECYCLE BIN.
WELL DONE, EVERYONE! LET'S ALL DO OUR PART TO KEEP THE EARTH CLEAN!

THE END

TRASH TALK

Think of the trash that you and your family generate at home on a daily basis. Now consider if some of that trash can be recycled. Objects made of glass, paper, metal and plastic can be recycled to make new products. For example, aluminium drink cans can be recycled by melting them down to make new aluminium products.

Trash collected from homes is sent to landfills, which are sites for disposing large amounts of trash. We can drastically reduce the amount of trash that goes to landfills by simply placing our recyclable trash in the correct recycle bins.

Objects made of glass, paper, metal and plastic can be recycled to make new products.

Recycling reduces the need to consume more natural resources. This can help to protect habitats. For example, if we recycle newspapers, fewer trees would have to be cut down to make paper. This would help protect many forests.

Recycling can help prevent natural resources, such as forests, from destruction.

Recycling also saves energy and slows down the rate at which landfills get filled up. This lowers the amount of harmful gases released into the environment.

Practising the three Rs — Reduce, Reuse and Recycle — can go a long way in saving our planet! Start today by reducing your waste, reusing things instead of throwing them away, and placing recyclable trash in the correct recycle bins.

TAKE THE CHALLENGE!

Another way to reduce the amount of trash we generate is to modify and use an unwanted object in a way that increases the original object's value. This is known as ______________.

- [ ] decycling
- [ ] upcycling
- [ ] freecycling
- [ ] downcycling

ANSWER: UPCYCLING

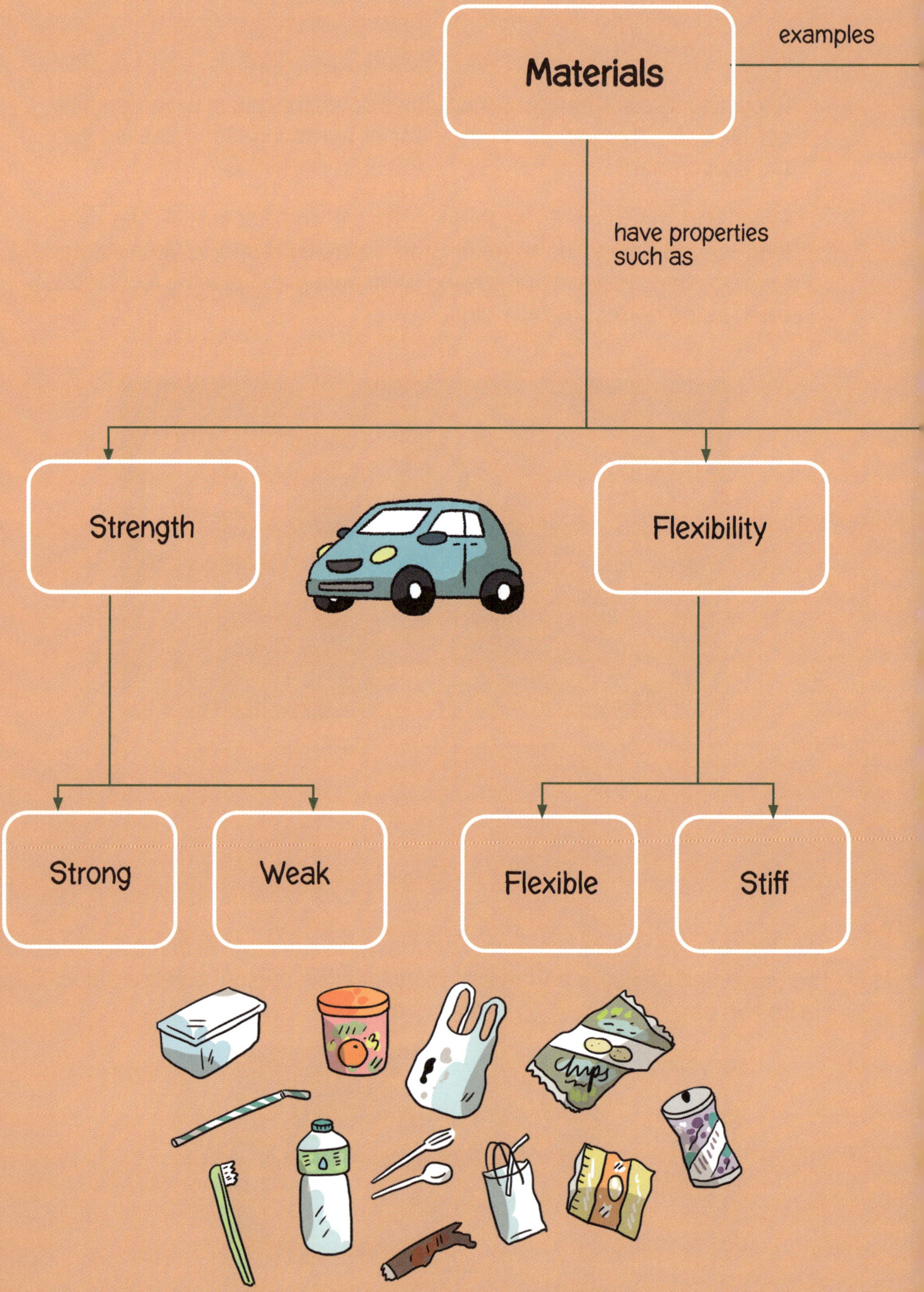
Materials
examples
have properties such as
Strength
Flexibility
Strong
Weak
Flexible
Stiff
chips

- Wood
- Metal
- Ceramic
- Rubber
- Glass
- Plastic
- Fabric

- Ability to float on or sink in water
  - Float
  - Sink
- Ability to absorb water
  - Waterproof
  - Not waterproof
- Transparency
  - Transparent
  - Translucent
  - Opaque

WANT TO TEST YOURSELF AFTER READING?
SCAN THIS QR CODE TO DOWNLOAD
PRACTICE WORKSHEETS!

READ MORE *SCIENCE CHAMPS!*